PECULIAR PETS

Green Iguanas

WITHDRAWN

by Natalie Lunis

Consultant: Nannette Gunn
Green Iguana Society Adoption Team

BEARPORT
PUBLISHING

New York, New York

Credits

Cover and Title Page, © Dave King/Dorling Kindersley/Getty Images; TOC, © rusm/iStockphoto; 4, © South Wales Evening Post; 5, © John Kaprielian/Photo Researchers, Inc.; 6, © blickwinkel/Alamy; 6-7, © Prisma/SuperStock; 7, © Huetter/blickwinkel/Alamy; 8, © Lourens Smak/Alamy; 9, © Oyvind Martinsen/Alamy; 10, © Ace Castillo; 11T, © Darry Conner; 11B, Courtesy of Green Iguana Society; 12, © Zigmund Leszczynski/Animals Animals Enterprises; 13T, © James Kuhn; 13B, © Emy Smith Photography; 14T, © D. Ross Cameron/Oakland Tribune/ZUMA Press; 14B, © domin_ domin/iStockphoto; 15, © Zigmund Leszczynski/Animals Animals Enterprises; 16, © Silvia Struve; 17, © José V. Resino; 18L, © Chris Radburn/PA Archive/Press Association Images; 18R, © Michael McBroom; 19, © Carl Palazzolo; 20, © Ayudya/Shutterstock; 21, Courtesy of Green Iguana Society; 22, © Stuart Westmorland/The Image Bank/Getty Images; 23, © Eric Isselée/Shutterstock.

Publisher: Kenn Goin
Editorial Director: Adam Siegel
Creative Director: Spencer Brinker
Design: Debrah Kaiser
Photo Researcher: Omni-Photo Communications, Inc.

Library of Congress Cataloging-in-Publication Data

Lunis, Natalie.
 Green iguanas / by Natalie Lunis.
   p. cm. — (Peculiar pets)
 Includes bibliographical references and index.
 ISBN-13: 978-1-59716-863-2 (library binding)
 ISBN-10: 1-59716-863-7 (library binding)
 1. Green iguanas as pets—Juvenile literature. 2. Green iguana—Juvenile literature. I. Title.
 SF459.I38L86 2010
 639.3'9542—dc22

                                                2009017545

For more information, write to Bearport Publishing Company, Inc., 101 Fifth Avenue, Suite 6R, New York, New York 10003. Printed in the United States of America.

10 9 8 7 6 5 4 3 2 1

Contents

Up a Tree

Debbie Davies was worried. She had taken her pet Rex for a little walk in her front yard in Swansea, Wales. However, Rex had wiggled his way out of his leash and climbed straight up a neighbor's tree. Now it was getting cold and dark outside.

Rex

Luckily, the rescuers Debbie had called for arrived quickly. The firefighters got Rex down from the tree. Then he was brought inside and given a bath. The warm water helped him recover from the cold outdoor temperature. Debbie breathed a sigh of relief. Her green iguana was back at home, safe and sound.

Debbie had taken Rex outside to find and collect dandelion leaves—a favorite iguana food.

A green iguana munching on some dandelion leaves

Long-tailed Lizards

There are about 650 kinds of iguanas. Only a few of them are kept as pets by people who love **lizards** and other **reptiles**. By far, the most popular kind of pet iguana is the green iguana.

Many people think that iguanas look like little dinosaurs or dragons.

Green iguanas have long bodies with very long tails. In fact, their tails make up about two-thirds of their total length. Like all reptiles, they are covered with **scaly** skin. They are also **cold-blooded**. That means that, like all reptiles, their bodies cannot produce the heat they need to stay alive. Instead, they depend on the heat from their surroundings.

The scales that cover a reptile are made of the same material as people's fingernails.

scales

crest

spikes

A green iguana has a crest made up of many small spikes running along its back.

In the Wild

Green iguanas are **native** to Mexico, Central America, and South America. They are found mainly in warm, leafy forests near streams or rivers. There, they spend most of their time in the trees, **basking** in the sun to warm up, and moving into the shade to cool down. Sometimes they also jump into the water when they want to cool off.

An iguana basking in the sun

Green Iguanas in the Wild

Where green iguanas live

Iguanas find most of the food they need in trees. The lizards eat leaves, fruit, and flowers. Many kinds of animals, including hawks, owls, and snakes, eat iguanas, so the large lizards need to keep watch for enemies as they search for food. Luckily, their green color helps them stay hidden in their leafy homes.

▲ Green iguanas are plant-eaters.

In the past, the green iguanas that people kept as pets were captured in the wild. Today, most pet iguanas are raised on iguana farms in Central America, Florida, and Texas.

Living Large

A full-grown iguana can measure 6 feet (1.8 m) in length. That's a lot of lizard! That's also why this pet needs a lot of living space.

A large branch inside an iguana's cage gives the lizard space to climb and bask in the sunlight.

Iguanas cannot live in places where the air is dry. Owners need to use machines called **humidifiers** to keep the humidity level of the air above 75 percent.

Many iguana owners use an entire room to house their pets. They place the very large cage that an adult iguana needs in a spot that gets plenty of sunlight. Near the cage, they place a heat lamp or other kind of heater. The heater keeps the temperature in the low to mid-90s°F (low to mid-30s°C) during the day—just right for an iguana. During the night, while the iguana sleeps, the temperature can be lower. However, it should not drop below 75°F (24°C).

sunlight lamp

▲ The glass in a window blocks UVB rays—which are one kind of light provided by the sun and which iguanas need to stay healthy. So all owners, even those who live in sunny places, need to add special "sunlight lamps" to provide the right kind of light for their pets.

11

Eating Green

In the wild, green leaves are a green iguana's main food. They are also its main food when it lives with people as a pet.

Kale, collard greens, turnip greens, and dandelion greens are some of the most healthful items that can go on an iguana's menu. Many owners mix them with chopped vegetables such as carrots, green beans, and squash to make a big green salad for their big green lizards.

Pet iguanas need to be fed at least one healthful meal every day.

Pet iguanas love lettuce—especially iceberg lettuce. However, **experts** call it the "junk food" of the iguana world. It might taste good to iguanas, but it has very few of the **nutrients** that they need. Iguanas also love fruits such as strawberries, peaches, and bananas, but these should be given to them as sweet treats rather than as main dishes.

◀ Iguanas should always have a big dish of fresh water to drink. The water needs to be changed daily because the lizards like to bathe in it, too.

Bananas make a yummy ▶
treat or snack.

Handle with Care

Iguanas are shy, **cautious** creatures. They are naturally afraid of larger animals that might grab and eat them. For this reason, people need to approach and handle them carefully.

◀ Iguanas should not be around young children, who might startle them or handle them roughly. They should be handled only by experienced iguana owners.

People who handle iguanas should wash their hands often. That's because an iguana, like many reptiles, can carry **bacteria** called salmonella (*sam*-uh-NEL-uh) in its **intestine** and its waste. People can get sick from salmonella when they get the bacteria on their hands and then touch their mouths.

Anyone who wants to tame an iguana—that is, teach it to be unafraid of people—needs to be patient and gentle. After all, no one wants a nervous, unhappy pet. Iguana owners need to be careful for their own sakes, too. Although the big green lizard would much rather run away or hide than fight, a really frightened iguana can bite and scratch to defend itself. It can also strike from the rear—swinging its long, heavy tail like a whip.

In the wild, iguanas use their tails as weapons against enemies that want to eat them—and against other iguanas that try to invade their space.

15

Starting Small

Experts say that people getting their first pet iguana should start with a baby. Young iguanas are easier to tame than older ones. They are more likely to get used to being around people, as long as the people work hard to win their trust.

A baby green iguana

A young iguana is ready to be brought home as a pet when it is three to five months old. At that age, it is one to one and a half feet (.3 to .5 m) long.

16

The best way to make friends with any iguana, whether it is young or old, is to give it plenty of time to be on its own. A few minutes a day of gentle handling is enough for the shy green lizards. Feeding the iguana treats by hand helps them get to know and trust their owners, too. Over time, these "baby steps" pay off. Many iguanas will recognize and possibly even crawl over to greet their owners after a few weeks.

▲ Iguanas learn to recognize people who care for them. They may run into a room to meet their owners when they hear their voices.

Training and Grooming

What can a tame iguana do? It can't do tricks like a dog or play chasing and pouncing games like a cat. However, it can climb up its owner's arm or leg and rest calmly on a shoulder. With the right training, it can also walk on a leash with its owner. It's a good idea, however, to first practice taking a stroll indoors or in a quiet, peaceful yard outdoors.

Iguanas like to rest on their owners' shoulders. ▶

A pet iguana out for a stroll

A tame, relaxed iguana will also be able to get the **grooming** that it needs. For an adult, that means having its **claws** trimmed about once a month. It also means something that is much more enjoyable for the water-loving lizards—taking a bath at least once a week.

Many owners wrap their iguanas in a towel when it's time to trim their claws. That way, they can pull out one leg at a time and keep the other legs from scratching them.

Who Wants an Iguana?

Most people wouldn't want a big green scaly lizard living with them. Others think green iguanas are interesting and lovable creatures and would gladly share their home with one. However, iguanas are not easy to care for. Anyone who wants one as a pet should be prepared to take on many **responsibilities**.

▲ Some owners who live in very warm, sunny places keep their iguanas outdoors.

Iguanas need to see a **veterinarian** once a year—but not just any veterinarian. Owners need to find a vet who knows how to treat reptiles.

For example, because green iguanas come from places with very warm **climates**, a pet iguana needs to be kept in very warm surroundings at all times. It also needs fresh, leafy food—not food from a can—every day. That's just the beginning. The big green lizard depends on its owner for everything. So, most of all, it needs someone who understands its personality and is willing to learn all there is to know about its plant-eating, sun-loving way of life.

Green Iguanas at a Glance

In some science fiction movies of the 1950s, iguanas were used to "play" dinosaurs.

Fast Facts

Weight: up to 25 pounds (11.3 kg)

Length: up to 6 feet (1.8 m)

Colors: usually bright green when young; grayish-green as an adult

Life Span: 15–20 years; sometimes longer

Personality: shy and cautious, though also somewhat curious; can learn to trust its owner if handled gently and patiently

Glossary

bacteria (bak-TEER-ee-uh) tiny living things that live in water, soil, plants, and animals, and may cause illness

basking (BASK-ing) lying in and enjoying warmth or sunlight

cautious (KAW-shuhss) careful and watchful

claws (KLAWZ) sharp nails on an animal's toes

climates (KLYE-mits) the typical weather in places

cold-blooded (KOHLD-*bluhd*-id) having a body temperature that changes with the temperature of the surroundings

experts (EK-spurts) people who know a lot about a subject

grooming (GROOM-ing) keeping an animal neat and clean

humidifiers (hyoo-MID-uh-*fye*-urz) machines that add moisture to the air

intestine (in-TESS-tin) a long tube-shaped body part inside an animal's belly that helps break down food

kale (KAYL) a leafy green vegetable

lizards (LIZ-urdz) reptiles with scaly bodies and, usually, four legs and long tails

native (NAY-tiv) naturally born and living in a particular place

nutrients (NOO-tree-uhnts) things that are found in food and needed by people or animals to stay healthy

reptiles (REP-tyelz) cold-blooded animals, such as lizards, snakes, turtles, and crocodiles, that have dry, scaly skin and lungs for breathing

responsibilities (ri-*spon*-suh-BIL-uh-teez) jobs; duties

scaly (SKAYL-ee) having scales, or small, thin plate-like parts that cover a reptile's or fish's body

veterinarian (*vet*-ur-uh-NAIR-ee-uhn) a doctor who takes care of animals

23

Index

Bibliography

Bartlett, Patricia, and R.D. Bartlett. *The Iguana Handbook.* Hauppauge, NY: Barron's (2000).

Flank, Lenny, Jr., ed. *The Essential Iguana.* New York: Howell Book House (1999).

Rosenthal, Karen. *The Iguana.* New York: Howell Book House (2001).

Read More

Landau, Elaine. *Your Pet Iguana.* New York: Children's Press (2007).

Miller, Jake. *The Green Iguana.* New York: Rosen (2003).

Simon, Elizabeth. *Caring for Your Iguana.* New York: Weigl Publishers (2005).

Learn More Online

To learn more about green iguanas, visit
www.bearportpublishing.com/PeculiarPets

About the Author

Natalie Lunis has written many nonfiction books for children. She lives in the Hudson River Valley, just north of New York City.